To Shelly & Peter
'Thank-you' *
friendship & support.

Summerlands
Pagan Death and Rebirth

Blessings & much
love to you both on your
journey.

John Awen

Take care.
John Awen

GREEN MAGIC

Green Magic
5 Stathe Cottages
Stathe
Somerset
TA7 0JL
England

www.greenmagicpublishing.com

Typeset by K.DESIGN
Winscombe, Somerset

ISBN 9780952767053

GREEN MAGIC

Foreword by
Barbara Meiklejohn-Free

'The art of living well and the art of dying
well are one.'

EPICURUS

In today's society death is a taboo subject. Rarely spoken
about, except in hushed tones, we avoid the subject at all
costs in case we summon up the Grim Reaper himself.
Every day thousands of people on the Earth are passing
to the Summerlands without assistance and support of
loved ones. Scared and frightened, they live out their
last few hours in the fear of the unknown without
anyone to assist them home. Our ancestors knew of a
different way of dying well. The cunning men and
woman of the Craft known as "sin eaters" lived within
our communities, helping those who's time it was to
pass over to the Summerlands. Their role as healers and
facilitators was to remove the sins and fears of those in
transition between the betwixt and between. As they
sang the dying person's soul back home to the isle of the

blessed, they were honouring a legacy passed from generation to generation as old as time itself.

Within the aboriginal cultures and traditions there is a rite of passage called "living through your death". This personal initiation helps each individual face and overcome the fear and terror of death ritually, so that each person can come to terms with the process of death with no fear. This rite of passage is fully supported by the elders of the tribe so that dying is no longer feared. Many other tribes and clans from around the ancient world revered death. Their realistic approach of integrating death and dying with everyday life, through storytelling of myths and legends, created a bond of unity and remembrance without separation of life and death.

The warriors of the clans and tribes of our ancient British Isles knew it was an honour to die well on the battlefield with no fears. Because of their deep knowledge of the cauldron of rebirth and it's magical properties they could face all adversities and foes knowing that they would be revived. They believed in reincarnation and the otherworld known as the Summerlands. This magical place, known to many as Annwn in Welsh mythology, is the resting place between incarnations. Here in this sacred place there is no pain or fear. There is an abundance of food and drink, there is no sickness or death. Can you imagine being raised on these stories by your kinsfolk of your tribe or clan knowing that when you did die in the physical form you would either be revived by the cauldron of rebirth or go to Annwn? You would have no fear of death and in a lot of cases welcome the journey in the never ending story of the circle of life.

Today in our so called advanced technology of quantum physics and deep space exploration, our ancient rituals and rites of passage for death and dying have been lost in the mists of time awaiting its rebirth. Only in the remote lands do these sacred rites of passage still take place.

Each of you reading this has a personal responsibility to ensure that this sacred art is not lost in the annuals of forgetfulness. John speaks to you through this book of his personal experiences and shares his own insights on death, dying and rebirth in an easy, readable manner.

I remember when my grandfather died. An old woman called Jessie appeared at our door. She was old and haggard and bent over but had the most amazing bright green eyes. She spoke with an Irish accent in a soft lamenting voice. She looked at me and said "You heard her in the middle of the night." I replied "Yes, who was that screaming and wailing?" "It was the banshee calling your grandfather home. Now get away with you, I have work to do."

She called for the death linen and my grandfather's best suit. She washed him, clothed him, singing a strange song in an unknown language. Then she was gone and in her place came all his family and friends who visited him in turn. Each one with a story of how he had made a difference in his or her life. There were tears and laughter as I watch my grandfather's whole life unfold in front of my very eyes. After three days of prayers, drinking, feasting at his wake, his family and friends left. It was at this point his spirit left the room. As I said goodbye to him (he had been sitting in his favourite chair the whole time) I noticed loads of letters inside his coffin. These were papers of regrets from those who felt they had not said their proper goodbyes to him. By writing their feelings and thoughts down they felt they had closure and completion, assisting him on his journey to the Summerlands without having ties to the earth plane because of unfinished business.

The rites of passage for death and dying in ancient cultures and traditions, up until very recently, were always supported by those who understood and knew how to transit through the veil of death. It was deemed sacred to assist and be in the presence of one who was dying. This was due to the spirits drawing close as the veils became thin for those transiting to the Summerlands, assisted by their loved ones on the Earth Plane and those in the Spirit World. This coming together of heaven and earth was done with the greatest of respect, honor, dignity and forethought.

Do you know that animals have no comprehension of what death is? Imagine if we humans did not have this fear of death. We could live out our lives fully embracing all life's ups and downs knowing that death is but a part of a process of the circle of life. Death, or the fear of death, separates us from the whole, the Divine "the I Am One with All that is".

Many of us who walk an Earth centred path experience first hand death and rebirth many times within one lifetime. John is one of those individuals who has died symbolically many times. With each death and rebirth comes an awakening and death of the ego's self importance. Many people, such as John, go through this process without knowing or comprehending why it is happening to them at the time it happens. Throughout the process of their death and rebirth there is a stripping down of the physical, mental, emotional bodies which assists in dying to the old self limiting belief patterns created through grief and trauma by others. This process makes way for new belief systems to be rewritten. This is very much like a computer which is constantly needing new software updates to function correctly. If this is not done on a regular basis the old programming will become infested with bugs and viruses closing the entire network down. This is the programming that most people live on throughout their lives. A slow painful fearful life.

When we experience death and rebirth, near death experiences, out of body experiences we become part of the matrix which reveals your life's journey as was shown to you before you came to the Earth Plane.

It's interesting to note that those who experience the profound near death experience or death and rebirth totally change their way of thinking, feeling of being a part of this world.

The Balams who were the priests of the Maya defeated death over and over again so that they could bring back the wisdom from the spirits who resided in the Summerlands. By acquiring the "Jaguar body" they were able to journey beyond death and return to the land of the living.

To die consciously you must harness your life force energy and focus this towards dying well. The ability to go back to the Summerlands in the state of awareness as when you were born is part of dreaming awake your spiritual essence into being.

What living legacy will you leave behind when you die? Will you be the whispering winds that inspire poets, artists and songwriters, the memories of sunsets and sunrises, of happy memories and joyful times, or will you leave this planet in a worse state than how you came in? The choice is yours to die well in your preparation to the Summerlands. Let the journey begin; only the destination is written, not the journey. In the words of Steve Jobs as he left this Earth Plane to make his transition to the Summerlands "Wow Wow Wow!"

Barbara Meiklejohn – Free The Highland Seer best selling and award winning Author of The Shaman Within, Book of Destiny and The Sacred Site Oracle Cards.

Acknowledgements

Throughout the time I have been writing this book, I have received support from so many people that it has been truly humbling and if I forget to include you now, I apologise.

Firstly, I would like to thank my Mum and Dad, both of whom have passed away, but are within my heart and inspire me every day. Without them both, I would not be here and who I am today. I love you both and thank you from the bottom of my heart. You are always with me.

Without any of the long lineage of ancestors that push us onwards from beyond the veil, none of us would be complete, so I honour you all and once again, I thank you.

To all my friends, a lot of whom have become Brothers and Sisters to me, simply because our friends are the family we choose, I thank you all and love you dearly. There have been countless friends whom I have asked for input, whether in person or by phone (they know who they are), when I have thought I was going mad. Such is the fun of writing a book, or creating anything at all, out of nothing. Thank you all so much.

When I was struggling to find inspiration and was unable to write a single word, a very special friend and Sister, Sam, gave me a loving family environment in which to create. From that moment, this book was begun and my inspiration flowed freely, much to Sam's annoyance at times, when I took over the kitchen table with all my clutter and made her listen to different sections of this book – even when she didn't want to, bless her. Love you Sam and thank you so much.

To everyone that has freely spoken to me on this subject and countless others who have shown and given me guidance, support and love: without you all, this book would not be what it is. Blessings and much love to you all. Always with me and friendships forged.

Special thanks to Barbara Meiklejohn – Free for her friendship, constant support and for writing the foreword for this book.

What is death?

This is the million dollar question – the proverbial Pandora's Box, so to speak. We all know that death is final (in this life, anyway). Whether it is a plant that dies off, or an animal, pet, or friend, we often watch a slow decline until they are no more. On the other hand, their death can be so sudden, instantly throwing our whole world out of kilter and into chaos, and we are left devastated. From this point on, we are often thrown into a world and existence of feeling robbed, with never-ending questions that only seem to bring more questions – most of which we are unable to answer. This then creates a huge void within us and we are left bereft and always wondering, why?

You may have noticed that I didn't mention the word 'family' in the last paragraph. This is because the majority of us think our families are invincible and will always be there. Our parents, siblings, aunties and uncles are our anchors throughout our younger and formative years: they keep us stable and so, until death happens within that unit, we assume that it will not directly affect us – if we actually think about it at all.

Within many cultures around the world, death is still celebrated and the deceased are honoured. Their lives are fondly remembered and an understanding and inner peace is often reached, albeit with extreme sadness, that this person has achieved and accomplished all they can in this life and have now journeyed onwards to another realm. On the other side of this, there are still a few cultures/societies where, naively, death is a massively taboo subject and is never talked about or recognised and is quite simply avoided and ignored. To think that this can happen is, to me, very sad indeed.

Let's look at this from a different perspective – one that is pragmatic and uncomplicated. This is not always easy to do, I know, but let's attempt to strip it down to the bare bones and assess this journey of death from a simpler way of understanding. By doing this, I am in no way detracting from what death is, what it means to us all, our individual interpretations, the grieving process involved how the loss of another hurts us and the immense suffering we can be left with. What I am going to attempt to do within this book is to offer the reader a different take on a topic that is really infinite and almost impossible to comprehend, until we take this journey ourselves. I myself have been pronounced dead more than once and have ventured into the realms of death many times. In fact, as I write this book now, I am in the early stages of heart failure. I have heart disease and several other severe complications within my own heart, so naturally, I have in the past reflected upon death and now meditate and visualise it every single day. This is a subject that fascinates me, but not in a morbid sense – believe me, I do not want to die, I am merely preparing and trying to understand this ultimate journey, which we are all embarking on from birth.

From beyond the veil we come…

Entering into another body vessel, once again arriving to continue our soul's path of learning, growth and evolution.

I absolutely believe that newborn babies often cry because they are so shocked to find themselves here, having left the warmth and comfort of the soul's stopover place that Pagans refer to as the

'Summerlands'. Imagine being in a realm of sheer beauty: here, there are no worries or stress, just a total connection to all that is – energy, life, the universe and all that is contained within. No negation to contend with, no oppression, just sheer and absolute harmony. This is the place where we truly and undeniably resonate. A place that is rooted deep within our DNA and our very essence. Wouldn't you cry, after arriving from paradise to here?

Obviously, after a while, memories of the Summerlands fade. We adjust to our new environment and then look forward with anticipation to what this life has to offer us. It's at this point that we are on the inevitable journey back to the Summerlands.

As I previously mentioned, many cultures across the world celebrate death, along with the whole transition of crossing over from this earthly plane into the Summerlands (or the equivalent). A realisation is reached: we come to understand that death is simply another part of the glorious cycle of life and is inevitable. Death is a time to honour, a time to give thanks for knowing and loving the deceased, for sharing and learning with them. Their journey ends, yes, but only the part of the journey in that body vessel that their soul and very essence inhabited for that time. I liken it to a never-ending train journey, a journey that keeps stopping at stations along the way. Like the train, our soul keeps moving onwards, but at each station we depart from the carriage to board another one. And so the journey continues.

The death of anybody is a sad event, but this is especially so when they are a family member or a much-loved friend. We grieve for them, we shed tears and often feel anger and immense frustration that they have passed on. All of these feelings and emotions are totally natural; they are also an intrinsic part of the grieving and healing process.

In the midst of all of this, we need to look within and ask ourselves: are we suffering a sense of loss for their sake, or for ourselves? This very question, when we are able to grasp and contemplate it, can prove pivotal as to our understanding of the whole process and the way in which we comprehend and deal with it. Obviously, at the time of losing someone we care deeply about, our thought patterns can become totally irrational; we can feel robbed, totally betrayed by what we may well view as something wrong and compelety unjust.

It's these feelings of bereavement – utter loss and sadness – that can often lead us to ostracise ourselves from everything else: family, friends, even our own feelings when they threaten to totally overwhelm us. This, unfortunately, is all too common and is invariably another part of the grieving and healing process.

The feeling of grief will ultimately occur. Indeed, it has to, simply for us to move on. Yet there is no time limit for this. Some may grieve for days, weeks, months, years – some may never move on and accept a loss and will grieve for the rest of their lives, such is the intense and immense pain, sadness and stress that they feel and become totally immersed and consumed by. No amount of words or comfort can ease them, for the situation is just too much to accept.

So, let me now ask the question and answer it from my own spiritual beliefs and personal experiences. 'What is death?'

The very word 'death' can make us feel uneasy and send us into shock and denial. It can send ripples through us, often signalling the end, finality and termination. Maybe if we could change our whole mindset and interpretation, then we would be able to flip the coin and achieve a much deeper, less hostile association with this word and all it represents?

If we look at the way in which everything works, we can see that everything is based on a whole; a process. This process is circular, a constant and is ever changing. However, within that, it starts and ends, thus bringing about a new beginning. The seasons that we see happening and feel around us like the dawning of the day are examples of this. We know that with these ever changing stages, there is a balance and a continuation. By viewing the seasons that encompass the earth in this light, we could liken spring to being born, summer could signify adolescence, autumn could be adulthood and winter could be the time of old age and ultimately death. With each of these passing times and seasons, we witness, appreciate and honour the new beginnings and endings. Once again, we just need to view the whole process as a natural one, as we do with the world as a whole. If we can view our own lives in the same way, it will surely be so much easier to come to terms with and accept – physically, mentally and spiritually.

As a Pagan, like many others, I celebrate the ever turning wheel of the year and mark each season with some form of celebration, ritual, or event. This can be simply giving thanks, having a fire, or decorating a home – maybe with the leaves, berries and fruit which are in abundance at that specific time. Within our own lives, we generally mark the turning of the year with birthdays and – if it's a milestone, such as a coming of age, or other important marker in our lives that is considered important – we celebrate, give thanks and honour the occasion accordingly. As I said, we can liken our lives and make comparisons with the ever-turning wheel of the year and the progression of our own lives. Thus, the seasons merely mirror our cycle of life and remind us that we are, all of us, in and of nature.

As a child, like most I suppose, I was led to believe that death – or passing over as I prefer to call it – was something to fear and try to ignore. This concept does not work; it shows us that if we try to conceal or ignore a topic then, when it does arise, we are not equipped to cope with it – nor any other emotion that surfaces with it. Nowadays, I know and totally understand that it is a time to remember that person fondly, to acknowledge and smile at the gifts that they and their lives showed us, and the joy that they brought; a time to carry them with us daily, within our hearts and our very being. If we can reach this level of understanding, then surely those who have passed are not dead; they become us and are part of who we are. They have simply moved addresses and we do not know the phone number on which to contact them. This does not however mean that we cannot speak or communicate with them. I speak with my parents, who have both passed now, every day and I feel them pushing me onwards and inspiring me in all that I do. It is my turn now to live my life, not just for me, but for them as well and for all of my ancestors who have gone before. Being in this mindset encourages me to be the best I can be and constantly stimulates me on all levels. It shows me that while I carry my loved ones in my heart, they are not really gone. This works for me and in my darkest times, it has brought me great comfort and strength.

On this 'train journey' to our ultimate destination in this body vessel, we should acknowledge, embrace and respect death, knowing that when we pass over, our soul is once again returning to Summerlands. Upon reaching that point, we can and will be reunited with family, friends and loved ones who have passed over and gone before. Try not to misunderstand me: I too have been left totally bereft and destroyed spiritually and emotionally by the loss of a loved one. I have wept uncontrollably and will again at the passing of a loved one. It is so painful and almost inconceivably devastating – the grief often becomes so overwhelming and consumes us totally. If we can flip the coin and view the positives, which do exist, then surely that's all for the better – easing both their journey and our own? Upon reaching this point of understanding and inner peace, then surely realisation awakens itself as well, ultimately making the passage of our loved ones into the other realms easier. This, too, should make our grief easier to understand, comprehend and become more at peace with.

Honour life and all creation daily, radiate love and good intentions. In living like this, we can attune our whole being on every level, hopefully reaching a much deeper and intrinsically spiritual understanding of the concept of the cycle of life and all of the wondrous joys it can bring.

Death is a time of transition; a time to rest, recuperate and recharge. We are all spiritual beings first and foremost; we are merely having and experiencing a human existence. This is all part of who we are, have been and will be. Without having these transitional periods, our souls would not learn and we would therefore be unable to gravitate towards what I believe is our ultimate goal: becoming the divine and ascended masters whom we are all capable of becoming. We must keep returning, learning, growing and evolving at each stage of life, until that becomes a possibility.

As I mentioned earlier, we are having a human existence. Our souls therefore inhabit different body vessels on each stop over point. Let's take a look at the soul: what is it and what drives it on? We are energy, and that is what the soul is – energy. Once created, energy is always there, whether it be in an object, or untamed and in the ether, it is constant and remains. Basically, once energy is created, it cannot be dispersed, nor dissipated. Our soul is on a journey of discovery, forever learning and evolving. This is our very essence, our core, our very embodiment. Our souls are what give our bodies the driving force: they push us onwards, often against the odds, and are the epitome of all that we are, our individuality and reside at the centre of our very heart and core. They are on a constant journey of discovery and evolution. Without a soul, we would simply not have energy and vitality; we could not exist as we do.

However we view the way we were created and the way in which we arrived as part of the universe living on this planet, does not matter – not now, anyway. We are able to imagine when our soul was first created – a blank canvas, for want of a better saying. Similar perhaps to a hard drive on a computer, that contains no programs and is ready for the operator to start using it.

So, here we have a soul, created from energy and ready to power a human body. Now we arrive at the point of birth. Obviously, this process is a little shocking. After nine months of floating around in a comfortable and warm place, listening to the steady throb of Mums heartbeat, we are suddenly thrown into what can only be conceived as an alien environment, where our senses – which have been somewhat cushioned in the womb – are now on serious overload. We now feel very vulnerable and out of the comfort zone in which we have been held for months.

Our soul is everything that we are and we do not recognise this fully and often take it for granted. Every single experience, no matter how small, is being

24

logged, stored and registered by our soul. Imagine a massive data bank of memory, stored within the universe – that, in a nutshell, is what our soul is. From the blank canvas, our empty soul, becomes an ever evolving picture, constantly storing and collecting data, from our life experiences. Good and bad, every single action is being recorded and becomes the blue print and carbon copy for exactly who we are. Not a single action is missed out or forgotten – not one. Let's say that, after around seventy years of age, our first soul's journey in a human body vessel ends and we die. What happens then?

We all know that upon death, or the expiration of our bodies, we can no longer function – this much is obvious. After a while, we are buried or cremated. The life force has left our body vessel – the soul has departed – so we cease to be. This is the point at which our soul crosses over to another world, plain, or realm. This is the realm that myself and many, many others choose to call The Summerlands. We have now technically passed away; we are dead.

Now let me try to explain what death is and what it means. Once again, I am writing this from my own views, beliefs, perspectives and experiences. This is still,

I understand, a very taboo subject and is extremely delicate to touch upon and explain, let alone to write a book about. There is no definitive evidence, so, as with many topics, this one is open to various interpretations, and this is mine.

Our soul, the blank canvas I spoke of earlier – has now completed its first outing; the first journey in a human body vessel. An unbelievable and incomprehensible amount of data has been collected within this new soul and is forming the very structure and core base of who we are. This information does not merely pertain to who we are within that first life's journey, but is providing the very blue print and map for all our other journeys. To even think about this, let alone attempt to comprehend it is absolutely mind blowing – so let's take it one step at a time. Hopefully, that will make it easier to understand.

As I mentioned earlier, the soul is made up of energy that cannot be destroyed, so upon its departure from a body vessel, where does it go? After taking on board and being overloaded with information, emotions, feelings, experiences, adventures and life in general, it is only fitting that this precious soul – our driving force – goes somewhere to rest and recuperate, as everything needs to from time to time. What better place for this vacation, so to speak, than in a beautiful environment, place so special and sacred that there is only love, harmony and splendour there. A place where anybody or anything can dwell and reside without negativity, oppression or sadness.

This utopian ideology does exist, and we have all been there. It's where we were created, have returned to and will return to again, simply because it's the place that our inner being, our soul, knows as home. Where better to return to after any journey than the place we feel most comfortable in – the very place we long and yearn for after any adventures. The very place that birthed us, gave us life and holds us within its very being and essence. Our soul's home, The Summerlands.

This book is taking us on a journey through different realms, different worlds and various levels of consciousness and unconsciousness. Some of these will resonate with you, some may not, but let's hope you can grasp most of which I am trying to explain.

Our soul has now departed from the body vessel which it inhabited on this earthly plain and has crossed over into a different realm, known as The Summerlands. This is home to us and is where our soul returns to recharge. Now, as I said earlier, the soul is our driving force and is the very essence and epitome of who we are – it is basically our everything. Without it we could not and would not be here.

Our soul has now returned home. As our soul is pure energy and has left the body vessel, we have also left behind our solid and mortal body along with all its confinement. Our energy is now unleashed, so to speak. Personally, I like to view this as a vortex, constant and always swirling, contained within its own field – invisible but there. Imagine swirling with no sight, smell, taste, touch – totally devoid of all senses – but within this realm, we do not need those earthly trappings, so we leave them behind when we depart our body vessels on earth. We do not need food, drink, light or dark here. We have crossed over simply to rest, recharge and wait for the time when we will board another train carriage and start another journey of discovery and learning.

Within this harmonious retreat and sanctuary, I believe that we have recognition. All those who we have loved on earth, our family, our friends and those we have been close with, are recognised and pulled together, like magnets that attract each other. I call this connection within the realm of The Summerlands, our 'Soul Tribe.' Here on earth, we have all experienced times when we recognise somebody but know that we have never had contact with, or met before. Well, this may help to explain that.

Our soul is now in the place it feels at home. It has already been on the most remarkable journey and on that journey, a vast and very expansive – almost infinite – amount of knowledge and learning has been accrued and taken on board. Now is the time to absorb all of that information, set it out much like a computer would, and assess and retain it all within the multitude of soul journey folders. This is the time when the soul can relax, be devoid of driving us onwards and simply relax within a place of total peace and recognition with family, friends and our Soul tribe.

How long our soul, our energy resides within The Summerlands, none of us can ever really know. This is because massive past-life regressions would be impossible to fully achieve, and we all reside at different levels of understanding and comprehension.

Our soul has now returned home and can rest, grow and evolve. Our very DNA and essence is contained and held firmly within our soul. We are all on a massive journey of infinite knowledge and exploration. I truly believe that we, as individuals, choose each life that we undertake before we even choose the body vessel in which we will inhabit along with our earthly parents. In my view, we decide and choose, when we will be born to earth, exactly who will raise us, the life that we will lead once we return here from The Summerlands. I know this alternate concept is not going to resonate with everyone, but it's a fascinating hypothesis and one that I truly believe in. It resonates within me whole heartedly.

Now at rest, our soul's computer database can absorb all of the information that it collected on its first life's journey. However we perceive or view this, it's mind blowing and extremely hard to analyse fully, let alone comprehend and understand. If we compare our soul's resting period to a computer going through updates and reboots, it does become a little easier to take on board. As I mentioned earlier, none of us can put a time scale on how long we are resting in The Summerlands. It could be days, months or years. The energy that we are whilst there does not comprehend, nor does it need to ascertain any length of time, because it is simply irrelevant and has no place there.

During this period of rest and transition, our soul remains our soul. However many lives we have and lead, our soul always returns to us, which ever body vessel we happen to take on and inhabit. We can compare this to chapters in a book. The different chapters link from one to another, building up a whole and complete story. We, as humans, are an infinite amount of chapters, but our journey and all of the experiences we have build up, albeit slowly, a whole book – it just takes an immeasurable amount of time to live that book.

Now we can look at what death is. I believe without a shadow of a doubt, that it is just the beginning – a time of rebirth, growth and evolution. As humans, we age and decay, some quicker than others, but whatever and however we perceive this, our soul does go on and on and on. We all know that our minds are infinite and scientifically, we are only beginning to scratch the surface on just how powerful they are. The soul, which returns to our various bodies time and time again, carries our very blueprint and every single experience we have ever had and will have. Take this to another level and try to imagine how powerful and infinite that is; surely the soul then becomes more powerful than the mind?

I believe that we all have lessons to learn in the many lives we have and will have. This is why we keep returning and will do again and again, until we can ultimately learn all there is to know. None of us can ever know what our ultimate destiny is, but I personally choose to believe that once our inner souls have become attuned with creation as a whole, when we can attain total empathy with all living beings and bare no prejudice or malice towards anything or anyone, then maybe – just maybe – we won't need to return. It will be at this point that we can rest forever, having learnt all that there is to learn. We could ultimately savour the innate beauty of the ultimate paradise: The Summerlands.

As I have previously mentioned, I am writing this book gathered and put together from my own personal Pagan beliefs (respecting, honouring and following the cycles of life, the seasons and the moon – all nature based) and also my own personal experiences. When I was born, in 1969, I came into the world with a chronic urine infection and severely under-developed lungs. Back then, these were life threatening conditions, much more so than they are today. I was swiftly taken away from my Mum and placed in an incubator, where I remained for almost four months. At this time, I was not expected to survive, but obviously I did. Since birth, death and near-death experiences have been prevalent in and around my life, it's no coincidence that I now find myself writing about this very subject.

My next encounter with death – in this case a deceased body – was when I was seven years old and an elderly auntie had passed away. I remember the upset in the family when this happened. I remember being taken to a place – I didn't know where it was, but for some reason I was taken to view the body in an open casket. All I remember is not wanting to open my eyes, as I was scared stiff of what would be visible. After seeing the motionless body laying there in a coffin, I was even more frightened of the word 'death', let alone the idea that it might happen to me one day. Maybe from this point onwards I picked up something that would stay with me for the rest of my life – who knows?

The people, we are now in this life are obviously not always who we have been. We live many lives in just this one lifetime, without even thinking about our previous and future lives. I have attempted suicide twice and have had to be resuscitated more than once. I have been involved in a stabbing – I was the person stabbed and had to receive a full blood transfusion. I have suffered heart attacks and have also had several serious operations. I have experienced the first stages of passing over on more than one occasion and I now find myself in the early stages of heart failure, with faulty valves, solidification of parts of my heart and heart disease. For these reasons, I think about death and my ultimate journey every single day. I have also worked within the funeral business, collecting the deceased, placing the bodies in caskets, dressing them and carrying the coffins into the crematoriums or lowering them into a grave. I have witnessed grieving families and relatives first hand at each stage of the process – I have comforted, spoke with and bonded with them. I have also viewed what happens within the burning room of the crematorium and ultimately collected the remains of the deceased. On my own personal journey, I have entered a friend's flat with a Police officer and found them dead. I have also witnessed several friends passing over and, as a Druid, have been asked on more than one occasion to perform full death rite ceremonies and passing over rituals. All of these events have moulded and shaped me and prepared me, I believe, for my ultimate journey – they have given me a more intrinsic and much deeper understanding of what death is, what happens and where we are going.

There have been three different occasions during my life when I have been aware of slipping away and each one of these times has been exactly the same. The following piece is my own personal experience of dying and, as each of them were the same, it's easy to recall.

A warm glow penetrates my very being and essence. I become aware of my physical body fading, slipping away and becoming weakened. It's as if I am slipping out of my skin, which effectively I am. As the waves of intense heat envelop and wash over me, I am aware of my surroundings, but they also appear and seem alien at the same time. I feel so at ease that there is no fear at all; it's a state that I am more than comfortable with. I am aware of lying down, but not on a hardened and uncomfortable floor – to say floating would be more appropriate. My whole being is highly sensitised, tingling and glowing all over. I am stripped now of all emotions and there is no fear at all, just total peace and intense comfort.

There is a lot more that I could say about what happened next, but now is not the time. I do not want to indoctrinate you with my experiences as I believe that all passing over times are different for the individual. I have spoken to many people who have slipped away and returned and, the experiences all differ, from person to person. I have also read scribbled notes from those who are now gone, explaining what has happened just before their own passing. It's an incredible and infinite subject and, no matter what we think about death and how we regard it, it is the one thing in life that is inevitable for all of us.

No matter our belief system or structure, I believe that whatever God, Goddess, or deity you follow will be there to ease, assist and comfort you when the time comes for your transition into The Summerlands, or whichever name you might have for that place of peace and comfort that we arrive in when we die and pass over into another realm.

Let's now bring together all that has been written here, albeit in a nutshell. What is death?

Death is not final, but a mere beginning – a time of transition where our soul departs the human body vessel it has inhabited since it arrived in this lifetime.

Another chapter written in the huge book that brings together the immense journey that is ours to write and learn from, to recall and savour. Everything we face while here is another part of our massive learning curve. Whether that is good, or bad, we should take it all on board, strip it down and face the consequences – for when it's our time, it is us who is ultimately responsible for our own actions and nobody else. A time of great sadness will follow for the loved ones, family and friends who remain behind; this is only natural and sadly, par for the course. For the deceased, a time of intense and immense joy will proceed, as now they are totally free of the ties that bind and hold them within this realm. The very essence, the soul, can now vortex freely and go and rest. Believe me, it will need this because in due course, it will return once more to continue the constant circle that is not death and dying, but an ever evolving and constant flow of birth and life.

"And the end of all our exploring,
 Will be to arrive where we started
 And know the place for the first time."

T.S. ELLIOT, FOUR QUARTETS.

Preparing for our ultimate journey

Every journey we stride out on and undertake begins with the very first step. Whether we embark on a physical odyssey, or a spiritual one, it begins in the same way. Once we are born into this world, we are undertaking a vast exploration – a journey so crammed and abundant that to even think about it in an instant is simply impossible to imagine, let alone recognize and appreciate fully.

From the time we arrive and are born, we are on a quest of learning. A plethora and multitude of sights, smells, sounds, tastes and other delights await us and tantalise our senses at every turn. A world of wonderful pleasures is there for us all to savour and enjoy, on all our conscious and unconscious levels. From the moment of birth, our driving force – our soul – is with us and accompanies us at every moment. For most people, what the soul is capable of and how much we work with it and rely and depend upon its guidance can be taken for granted.

As we embark on another chapter of our soul's journey (each life we have is part of this), every single person is on a different level of consciousness and unconsciousness. This level depends on how many times we have arrived here on earth, how much we have learnt and whether or not we actually connect with our inner self, our soul. Now this may sound totally absurd and you may well ask, how can anybody not connect with their own soul? Obviously, for anyone to live truly and connect with the universe as a whole, we need to link with our souls – otherwise we are not living as is intended and, within this, we are not really learning and absorbing the lessons we require to graduate to another level.

As a youngster, I was always aware of something – a presence within me and often around me – but I was unable to explain, let alone comprehend it. Because of this, I didn't question it and, in a sense, I suppose I ignored it and switched off from it. This will be the case for many people and when you consider why we do this, it's obvious really. Here we are living our life and then suddenly, our inner self, our soul appears and totally throws us out of kilter. It makes us sense and feel all we know in a different way and basically removes us from the comfort zone we are enveloped in. As humans, we take a lot for granted – we can become nonchalant and, at times, almost ignorant as to what really matters. To have our souls awakened and stirred can be extremely intimidating and at times almost frightening. For the purpose of this book, I will refer to our soul being awakened as a realisation, or an awakening. The following relates to my own journey and realisation of a different level of consciousness and my soul's awakening.

In 2007, I was thirty-eight years old. The life that I lived back then was different from the life that I lead now. As previously mentioned, we not only have different lifetimes, but we also lead and have many different lives within this one. It was getting into late summer of that year and I was walking with a friend. We were both chatting away in our own little world and the rest of the day was happening around us. Looking back now, I heard footsteps from behind, but didn't associate anything with it. The next thing I knew, my shoulder hurt and I became aware of being punched three times. A slight scuffle ensued and the person who had punched me quickly ran off. I instantly felt a bit faint and there was a lot of pain. The friend I was with looked at me in horror and it was at that point

I realised that what I had felt were not punches, but knife wounds – I had been stabbed three times. There was a lot of blood, obviously, down my back and legs and a pool was starting to form around my feet. At this point, I knew I was in trouble. I collapsed onto the floor and remember clearly to this day the taste of ash and dirt in my mouth as I started to fade away.

The feelings and flowing waves of intense but comforting warmth were so beautiful and I had no fear at all, just total and utter comfort. A million thoughts crossed my mind as I ebbed away, but the one prominent and most powerful thought that I had as I lay there, was 'There must be more to life?'

I had no idea what to do, but I totally believe it was this thought that kept me going and would ultimately change the person I was and mould me into who I am today. I don't remember any more, but needless to say I was taken to hospital, received a transfusion and left after a couple of weeks. From this point on, the way I viewed the world, all creation and the universe had changed. This was my own personal realisation and awakening.

I have spoken to many people about their experiences of arriving at this point and they are all different, obviously. It's not how we get there, but more to the point, that we do.

Life does not come with a manual. Even though there are rules which have to be adhered to, none of us are infallible and we make mistakes, we do things which can be construed as – and at times are – simply wrong. It is not up to any of us to cast aspersions and judge one another, but simply to hope that we can all learn and evolve from it. Within this very concept a realisation can take place that causes our soul to stir, thus setting us onto a truer and more enriched path, all of which stands us in good stead and paves the way for the individual preparation of the ultimate journey – death, or passing over.

If and when we become awakened, we are then in touch with our souls. This can be extremely daunting to start with, as we are basically removed from our so called comfort zones but then, within that, we are placed in the most comfortable zone there is. We become reunited with our true selves and connect with our real selves-much like a blanket that is familiar to us, we just have to recognise and re-connect with it.

Once we hopefully reach this point, we are then catapulted into what can only be described as viewing and seeing the world in its true sense. Our senses become heightened and our perception, compassion, sympathy and total empathy enters a whole new level. We now transform into what can only be described as a higher state of consciousness and awareness – physically, mentally and most of all, spiritually. It's as if a cloak or shroud has been torn and ripped away. We can feel totally vulnerable as the world and all it has to offer is suddenly viewed in a totally different and more sensitive way. Believe me I know and recognise how naïve this state can be and the emotional affect it can have on us. It's like everything we know has changed and almost becomes so awakened that we attempt to shy away from it. Well, that is not possible – once it has stirred and awakened, this heightened state of awareness will not leave us. We just learn to work and walk with it, using it for the greater good and benefit of the universe and ultimately, ourselves.

This state of awareness, the heightened state of perception – how we see, view and sense everything is – I believe, the totally natural consciousness of our soul. If we can attain this, then we are living in harmony and complete balance with all creation and are therefore closer to whatever Gods/Goddesses/

deities whom we look towards for guidance and inspiration. By living closer to them, we must surely be making preparations for our own ultimate journey?

There are many tales and stories about what happens at the moment of death – the feelings, emotions and the transition that may or may not happen. All these experiences are completely individual and, as I mentioned earlier, that's how I see it. We are all different, on different levels of understanding and connectedness with our surroundings, one another and all of creation. What I have tried to do within this book is to give my own experiences and beliefs regarding this still very taboo subject. I am a spiritual being, so I have given this from my spiritual mind and being.

There is balance in everything – there has to be. If we look around at all of creation the sacred and harmonious balance is contained everywhere we look. Love and dislike, male and female, dark and light, etc. Within our very cores and essence, we are made up of all these varying balances and it is up to each one of us to embrace what is contained within, recognise all aspects of ourselves and, then to harness and work with the energies to live and lead a spiritual and balanced existence. Only when we understand what and who we are, including what we are capable of being and manifesting on both sides of the scales, can we live justly and truly.

Even if we are lucky enough to live a spiritual life, this does not come overnight. Like anything, it has to be felt, worked with and understood. This can take a lifetime, simply because it is ongoing and we are forever learning, growing and evolving. In this life, we only get the one chance, so surely we have to live and lead the very best life that we can?

Upon our point of death, or passing over, I do not believe that we will be judged by another. The judgement will ultimately come from within ourselves. We hold our own souls, which are the map and record of all that we are now and will be. When faced with death, it is our own conscience; our own guilt and anxiety that will make us turn away from entering The Summerlands, if we do not see ourselves as worthy. Surely then, if we get the chance to adjust the way we live, then we simply must embrace it and work with it all to live a more harmonious life. All of this will then stand us in good stead for our own selves and our ultimate journey of passing over.

Imagine if when confronted with all this, we have not worked on ourselves and still carry guilt and shame. Then, like a child, we will not be able to hide this, as our life force, our soul, will be on display for the universe and spirit to feel and sense. This is where, like a child, we would naturally shy away from passing over into the most beautiful and tranquil place that we can ever imagine. Having just the one shot at this, for me, the very thought of shying away and maybe going somewhere else is simply not an option. As I said earlier, I have made mistakes as we all have and, over the years, I have worked hard to change the person I was. I now live what I consider to be a spiritual life. By doing this, I believe that I am making preparations for what will eventually be my ultimate journey.

Other preparations we can put in place are more physical: writing a will, letting family and friends know about our final wishes, etc. I will include a section later outlining what we do when a death occurs, with contact procedure and other information. All of this is important and is handy to know at a time that is immensely stressful and harrowing, both emotionally and spiritually.

From beyond the veil we come

Entering into another body vessel – once again arriving to continue our soul's journey and path of learning, growth and evolution.

After an immeasurable amount of time, our soul, after its rest in the Summerlands, eases itself and is awakened once more into another body. We are born again and are ready to start another journey of discovery, awareness and enlightenment – another chapter, so to speak.

An amazing transformation now takes place. It is from this point that our soul is reignited into life and the very spark that drives us on, the very essence of life itself – our soul – continues and embraces all there is. Try to imagine what it must feel like to suddenly be catapulted from a place so serene and peaceful, into a world where all of our senses are suddenly working on overload. It's no wonder that some babies start to cry – wouldn't you? If we look at the two types of babies that arrive into this world – those who cry and those who do not with a vague hope of understanding their behaviour, then it becomes easier to comprehend.

I believe that babies who cry when first born, may well be relatively new souls and are not yet accustomed to life here on earth – well, that's my understanding of it, anyway. As I said earlier, suddenly we are thrust into a world of sights, smells, sounds and a multitude of other sensory alerts – it's no wonder that this trauma makes us a little bit upset.

Upon arriving here, we have basically stepped through what I call the Veil, the invisible curtain which separates the realms of this life and the afterlife – the shroud, or cloak that partitions those passed from those who are living. For a short time, we still contain memories from the Summerlands. These obviously fade fairly quickly once we are birthed and are soon erased from our consciousness and transported into our sub consciousness, or our soul. Although an awareness of these memories is re called at times – through soul journeying, meditations and times of awakening – we're often unable to place where we know them from. This is another trip switch that we carry, simply to avoid our physical and mental selves being overloaded –it is a form of protection and self preservation.

A fairly, or relatively new soul arrives and almost at once, it realises that a massive transition has occurred – a state of sublime awareness has suddenly become a huge overload on their very being and their whole state of awareness is now potentially under attack on all levels. Not only is the soul awakened once more, which is extremely daunting and can be highly intimidating (especially for a relatively new soul starting out once more upon its journey), but an enormous state of consciousness takes shift from this moment. A realisation of the fact that our soul, is now embodied within a vessel comes into play here. Rather than being the swirling vortex, which we were in the Summerlands, we are now encased within a body vessel. This must be so very intimidating, restrictive and oppressive, especially after our time of rest in a place of beauty and total peace.

If we can even slightly grasp this, then it really does become clear as to why some babies cry upon their arrival into this earthly realm, or plain.

Now let us take a look at the babies that are born and do not cry. My interpretation and comprehension of a newborn baby that does not cry upon arrival, is an older, more matured and enlightened soul. We have all seen or heard of babies that do not scream, but are instead content with this re-birth and the environment around them which they suddenly find themselves part of and encapsulated within. This could be seen as a phenomenon, but I think it's easier to liken this to a soul that has journeyed here at least several, maybe many times before. To me this shows that whatever stage or part of our soul's evolution we are at, there are many different and varying levels of our conscious being, as well as our subconscious being, our soul.

Upon our soul's departure from the Summerlands, our time here is spent on a trajectory of birth, life and all the experiences and lessons we have waiting for us, which I believe we chose and saw the blueprint for long before we arrived and decide on our next body vessel. To comprehend this can be extremely daunting and at times overwhelming, but if we break it down, as I have tried to here, our grasp of this becomes so much clearer and easier to understand, work with and acknowledge.

We now find ourselves born onto and into this world. Everything here is available for us and is geared to sustain us on all levels: physically, mentally and spiritually. Depending on the stage of our soul's development we have reached, we now have the opportunity to progress further on our journey. All the sensory stimulation that we need is readily available and on tap – it's just up to us as individuals to awaken our essence, our very being, our soul and to continue our progression on the soul's journey.

Chapter by chapter, (lifetime by lifetime,) we seek soul tutoring and spiritual growth. Each time we return, invaluable lessons will be gained, achieved and taken on board and deep within our soul. All of this learning will eventually, I believe, help us achieve the reason for our being here in the first place. To reach spiritual enlightenment, which is the state of higher perception and an intrinsic understanding and knowledge of the life that is held inside the universe, then we once again must embrace all that we are, learn from all of the lessons we have experienced and understand within ourselves, just what we are here to do. This is totally achievable for us all and makes up the path of total enlightenment which is contained within us. To assist with any kind of spiritual path, or belief, we must first of all look at the bigger picture, which includes working with and attempting to understand the ways of the universe and what is expected of and from us.

As newborns, whether we cry or not, we are on a very magical journey of surprises and emotions, all of which encompass our soul's journey and odyssey of infinite learning. We choose the life we lead long before we arrive here on this beautiful earth and then, once we have arrived, our physical life ensues and another chapter which makes up the soul's book is continued once more, as from beyond the Veil we come.

We are them, as they are us

As each one of us stands here today, we are made up of a multitude of others. Our ancestors, parents, family, friends and all life that has existed since time began are tightly bound and entwined deep within our psyche and DNA, making up our life force and constantly pushing us onwards. As well as having our soul's infinite knowledge, lessons and guidance while we journey through each lifetime, we are also inspired and driven by the universe and everything contained within it.

Imagine, if you can, an invisible spider's web, that covers not only this world, but also enshrouds other worlds, realms and life forces – basically an infinite lineage which abridges not only everything that we can comprehend, but a vast array of so much more. From the very first spark, or breath that infused the world, the universe and all of life and creation as we know and see it, we have been put on and placed on a cataclysmic journey of discovery. This journey has been infused and installed deep within our very essence, molecular structure and each strand of our very existence. It forms who we ultimately are, have been and will be again.

I understand that the very concept of this is mesmerizingly mind blowing and extremely hard to grasp, let alone absorb and take in. However, to understand ourselves – to realise who and what we are, how we came to be and our very lineage of existence – we have to attempt to grasp this. If you take a piece of wood and sand it down until you have a huge pile of sawdust – a pile which is impossible to contain, let alone count the dust particles – this may give you an easier understanding of what and who we are and how we stand here now. Imagine, as you gaze up into the night sky, the sheer and utter power, force and limitless vastness there is; now we can maybe begin to understand what we are and all that stands within, alongside and around us.

I don't know if you will be familiar with the words 'Akashic records'? This is terminology used within theosophy and anthroposophy and is the word used to explain the vast compendium of thoughts, events and emotions that is encoded and makes up all of the knowledge and events that have ever taken place within the universe, since time first burst into fruition. Basically, this is the blueprint and data bank archives of everything: every action, thought, intent, being and everything else we can think of (and those that we can't). We have all had that moment when we're familiar with a place, or are able to explain something while being fully aware that we have not been there or have never read about or learnt that particular subject. These are the moments when our soul, or our mind taps into the Akashic records and fuels us with the information that we are seeking and wish to know and understand. The sheer vastness and infinite supply of information that is available for each one of us to connect to and use is incredible and impossible to fathom out. Because of this, it then becomes one of those issues that we must simply go along with, work with and follow with our heart.

Now, if we compare the Akashic records to who we are and how much we have contained within our very being, then we can start to maybe not understand, but appreciate and respect it whole heartedly. I called this section of my book, 'We are them, as they are us,' because for me, it gave a deeper thought and concept of what I am attempting to explain within this section. I could have called it many different things, but I was also hoping to invoke thought in the wording, which hopefully I may have achieved.

We are all spiritual beings who are merely having a human existence once again. We will go on and continue to do this until, maybe one day, we have totally consumed and become part of the vast data bank of infinity, reaching a harmonious and empathic state of consciousness and understanding with such an attuned and intrinsic level of comprehension, that we no longer need to return – who knows?

Let's return now to the subject in hand. Hopefully we can now see and understand, albeit on a small and scaled-down level, how ingrained our existence is with every being who has ever lived and each action that has ever taken place and come into manifestation throughout the universe and time itself?

On this magical and vast journey that we have each undertaken and are on, we do not live our lives just for us – that much is obvious and very plain to see. We are living this life and each one we have for all of our ancestors, our friends, family and everybody that has ever been in existence. Now, we have strong and infinite connections to those who have installed time, energy and love upon and within us. I termed this connection earlier as Soul tribes, just so you know what I mean when I speak of those close to us.

The vastness of the invisible spider's web that epitomizes and is gently laid across the immense and many worlds and realms that make up this existence cannot really be imagined, but it is there. Contained within that web are an infinite number of threads and various strands. Like ripples when we cast a pebble into fresh waters, they spread and are felt by all of creation, often subconsciously. However, very often, once we do connect and are attuned on a different vibrational level, we can sense, feel and just know when a shift takes place, however small it may seem. This shows us all how much we are part of the bigger make up of the planet and universe in which we live and exist. Maybe now, we can perceive that we do not stand alone, but are constantly guided, nurtured, loved and inspired by those we walk with and live for now. They strengthen us on our life's journey and gently embrace us in all that we do.

Condensed within us, we can maybe now see that we have a plethora of ancestors and guardians that walk, live and enjoy life with us every day and we are living for these precious souls as well, as for our own being and path of knowledge, wisdom, growth and learning. The warm hand of comfort we feel when we feel lost or saddened: the drive and inspiration we feel when we need encouragement, or do not know which way to turn; in times of pain and sorrow, loss and confusion, the warming embrace or comforting words we feel on the breeze – this is them and their presence goes further to demonstrate the connections that are there. They cannot be denied and should be savoured, embraced, worked with and viewed as a huge gift from our guardians and protectors.

We can very often, become complacent with life, with our outlook and we can also invariably take things for granted. We all do – it's not that we should, it's just that we do. Once we become awakened spiritually, then our conscious and unconscious states of awareness burst through into being and come into fruition. Upon this awakening, our very essence, our soul is stirred into life and becomes a part of our understanding and arrives at the forefront of who we are and how we perceive and act towards life itself, and towards any given situation that we find ourselves in or may be confronted with. It is from now on and with this enlightenment that our lives become whole and complete for all our levels of being, physically, mentally and spiritually. We are then able to call upon the universe and our ancestors for guidance, strength and much, much more. We can seek comfort, insight, foresight and wisdom from them all, as and when we need it. To have this universal font of all knowledge there, basically on tap and available to us, is humbling and, on the grand scale of things, simply mind blowing.

This book is not just about how I see, view, perceive and walk within the realm of death, or passing over. It's also about how I personally see our encompassment with the universe and life as a whole. Within this very concept, I believe that we must journey into all of the realms and other worlds that make up all that we are, simply to attempt to understand and get a grip on all of this. How can we have, or give a valid opinion on a subject that we have not looked into, witnessed, or experienced? We can't, it is from my own beliefs, my personal experiences and working with my own deep-seated spirituality that I have written this book and presented it to you. Obviously, as with any subject, it is totally open to interpretation and understanding, but I hope that somewhere within these words, I may have touched, reached, comforted, or maybe even inspired you?

On my own life's journey, I have had several experiences of passing over. I have personally slipped over into the realm of death and I have held animals and comforted them as they make the transition into the Summerlands. I have worked within the funeral trade and have also lost family members and close friends along the way. I am no expert on this topic – who could be – but I have so many experiences of this subject I felt that this book was screaming to be written. I have called upon my own experiences, those of others and all of my ancestors to give you my take and interpretation on this unfortunately still taboo subject.

Death, or passing over as I prefer to call it, is not the end and never will be. It is merely a new beginning and another chapter that has to be written. I am not, in any way, shape, or form, detracting from how extremely devastating and sad the loss of a loved one, family member, or friend is. I am only too aware of the immense sadness and burden which this presents, and always will. I am merely attempting to give a pragmatic take on what can be seen as a very difficult and highly emotional subject, along with a different viewpoint upon it.

Standing here now, as each one of us does, we are on the cusp of new learnings, new understandings and a whole new life's journey. We must never assume that we are here alone because, as I have explained and you will all be aware of anyway, we stand here with a multitude of others, incorporating our ancestors, family members since time began and all other beings that might wish and want to join us on our intrepid venture throughout this lifetime.

If we view all these beings, as people we can call upon in times of need – whether that is for strength, guidance, etc. – it becomes easier to comprehend and understand. Many cultures, tribes and beliefs often call upon what a lot of us refer to as 'Guides.' These beings will often willingly come and guide us. Throughout the ages, seers, clairvoyants and other various mystics have openly called upon their guides to help out and assist with insights, problems and foresight. Unfortunately, a lot of these have been (and still are) charlatans exploiting the vulnerable, but that is another thing totally. We must not detract from the fact that any one of us can call upon these guides at any time, for a great deal of assistance and comfort. We are not alone in this life and no matter what our belief system or structure, we are all aware of this fact.

To round this off now, I sincerely hope that I have offered you an insight into the way in which we stand here as a vast array and collection of individuals, simply because we hold the spirit of our lineage and ancestors who have gone before us. This makes us a collection of all these souls, who have now passed away. We just have to accept, embrace and utilise these guides at times when they come forward of their own accord, or when we call upon them for guidance, strength, wisdom and knowledge.

Accept the universe as it is, along with all of the wonders that it has to offer, even if we cannot always see, or understand them. The various realms and worlds around, which are infinite, will lend themselves to us to assist, comfort and guide us on our life's journey. Messages and signs should be recognised for the good that they can bring and adhering to them is vital as well. We must remember that these guides, beings and entities are all around us constantly and have unlocked the secrets of the universe – how it works and how we can best become attuned to it for the greater good of all life and, within that, ourselves. They have lived their lives and we should respect the comfort, solace and guidance that they offer us. Remember, we are them, as they are us.

Encompassing the universe and working with our own divinity

JOHN AWEN

To encompass the universe is literally to embrace and work with it as a whole. Now, I understand that some of you may well be questioning my reasons for putting this section into a book which is predominantly about our journey to death, or passing over. What I am trying to do here, within these pages and especially this section, is to encompass and give an interpretation and reasoning into a picture that incorporates the complete journey of our arrival here. I believe that in doing so, we may find it easier to understand how we might attain completeness within our spirituality and achieve the ultimate goal, which is surely to become the divine beings that we can be.

Once our journey starts, we embrace many lifetimes – we have to. This is because we are on a path of learning and unfortunately, due to our human bodies only having a relatively short life expectancy, we have to return again and again to nourish and feed our soul with all of the lessons that are there for us all. Without under-standing and comprehending all that there is to absorb and take in, surely it would all fall flat and our journey would become relatively pointless?

Every journey we take, or venture out on, begins with the very first step. Each time we are reborn into this world, another chapter of our soul's journey starts. If we can learn to embrace everything, encapsulate all there is and harness the guidance which is all around, then we can hold it within and gradually progress to another level of spiritual learning. This is all part of encompassing the universe, which in turn helps us to explain the bigger journey of being born again and again and returning to the Summerlands, the vital place of rest and recharge for our soul.

Throughout many cultures across the world, we see various groups and individuals whom adhere to the codes and beliefs of working, or encompassing the universe. These people are sometimes called Shaman, Druids, Wiccans, or Witches, Clairvoyants, Seers and a variety of other eclectic names. Many cultures have, throughout time, looked towards figureheads within their community, villages and tribes. These individuals are often perceived as wise men/women and have been (and in some places still are) looked towards for guidance, healing and a multitude of other advisory perspectives.

From a completely pragmatic and rational perspective, certain factions and solitary people have, throughout history been sought after to give insight.

Examples of the kind of information supplied by these people includes the foresight into daily activities and in the longer term, the outcome of crops, as well as of people's lives in general.

Once again, within this there will always be the charlatans who do nothing more than exploit others. However, there also exists those whose foresight is undeniable and ascends what most of us can understand. I am not going to start naming anybody, but if we look around the world at some highly popular individuals and the messages that they give, we might start to see that some of them are encompassing all of the lessons the universe has to offer. I believe that these highly attuned people are souls that have visited this earth many times and have, or are, achieving guru or living deity status. Their perception of life and all that it has to offer is just incredible and so highly tuned that I believe they could be termed as divine beings.

This section, will hopefully provide an insight into why we return from beyond the veil many times and how we can nurture, understand and work within our place in the universe. In doing so we are viewing the journey of death as a whole picture by looking at some different aspects of this taboo and difficult topic.

The very word 'Divine' conjures up many thoughts and sadly, a lot of people tend to almost shy away from it. Divine literally means Godhead, deity, ascended being and also soul. There are a great many other interpretations if you look, but for this piece, I am happy with this explanation.

Divinity can often be interpreted as not of this world, but I question that outlook. As I mentioned before, there are a few beings whom I personally consider to have transcended any so called 'normal' way of teaching and understanding of the kind that we relate and associate within our everyday lives here on earth. When studied and observed, even from afar, these people are so in tune with the universe – attuned on such a deep and intrinsic level – and have reached such a deep level of conscious awareness that they are, to me anyway, divine beings.

This altered state can only be achieved when our conscious and unconscious minds lower their vibrational level, therefore allowing us to connect to a much deeper state of awareness – physically, mentally and spiritually. If we can achieve this level of being then we will surely be living in what I can only term as a harmonious lifestyle, which is definitely the level we should all be striving to reach.

Several stages have to be in place for this ultimate awareness to be achieved, alomg with many, many lifetimes of learning and hard slog. Your whole state of mind would need to shift to reach this point, which, as I said, would take many lifetimes and a total and utter connection with the universe and all that is contained within this is a very slow and gradual process which, through deep meditation and many lives, can be established. The way we think, see, sense and feel would change dramatically – it would have to.

We are now talking about beings that become so utterly complex that their whole molecular structure (DNA) is changed. Their mindset is irrefutably remodelled and remapped, thus allowing such an enormous and total change to take place. A very good and dear friend of mine once said to me that I should stop listening to the incessant and constant nagging that goes on in my head – all of us will know what I mean by this. The next step from this is to start thinking and feeling from the heart which, to begin with, does not come automatically, or overnight. I practiced this and I have to say that it works and has proven invaluable to me on my path and my journey through this lifetime.

This process enables the gradual lowering of our whole vibrational level which, in turn, puts us on a path that may allow us to reach the next level of awareness and harmony. A different way of viewing everything inevitably comes with this and our lives undoubtedly become easier from this point. Please do not think that I am saying that I am a divine being – as I know I have many more lifetimes to go through yet – but we have to start somewhere. As I have said previously, every journey that we undertake starts with the very first step, so what better time to start making changes that will hold us in good stead through this lifetime and may well help us in our future ones as well?

Now this is a truly fascinating subject and concept – one which I could so easily delve into a lot more and certainly to a greater depth – but I believe I have explained, in laymans terms, what a divine being is, or could possibly be. What I am attempting and hopefully succeeding in doing throughout this book, is giving an interpretation of death and a lot of aspects that are associated within it. From a spiritual perspective, I have tried to ascertain all the relevance of not only death, or passing away, but also the way in which we can perceive and view it. By doing so, I hope to encompass a vast array of perspectives, not only of passing over, but also the many levels of awareness that we can hopefully achieve along our path – that if not in this lifetime, then in the other ones we shall find ourselves journeying into and through.

Allow me now to bring this section to a close. In doing this, I am going to connect the earlier part, in which I discussed the idea of encompassing the universe with the later section on the Divine, or Divinity. You will have noticed, I am sure, that within each section, I have gone off on a tangent at times, breaking down parts of the process that need reiterating and explaining. This is simply to give a deeper understanding of what we may expect to find and some of the processes which I believe playout when we do pass away. Obviously, this will be a massive undertaking and I can only hope that I may have eased any fears you might have been harbouring about this journey that we all find ourselves on.

If we can achieve an inner peace, a total calm – almost a constant meditative state – then I fully believe that we can reach a level of depth, attunement and resonation not only within ourselves, but also within the universe and all its workings. At this point, possibly after several lifetimes of working closely and in total harmony with all creation, then we may well become a living divine being. We are only held, or bound by the restrictions that we place upon ourselves and we only have to look around the world at some of the incredible, intuitive beings – wise beyond any normal comprehension – beings that are there. We can all attain this state of being; it just takes a long, long time and a heightened and constant state of awareness. Nothing is impossible.

Once achieved, this state will then become a constant – physically, mentally and, of course, spiritually. The universe will then lend itself to us, therefore assisting and allowing us to feel, sense and explore all that there is to know. At this point, it is possible that we have achieved, or at least recognised the divinity we are all capable of having and becoming. We are also ready to further follow, investigate and work closely (and as one) with the universe. Therefore, we have encompassed the universe and are working with our own divinity.

What are the Summerlands?

Once we have returned back to the Summerlands, we are without our earthly form and all that comes with it. We find that all the restraints and constraints that held us on the earthly realm are now gone, and we return once more to the swirling vortex that is the energy field of us. An immense change and shape shift has taken place as we go back to rest and recharge once more.

At this point, we are no longer bound by the feelings and emotions that all come as part and parcel of the earthly and mortal coil. We lose our human senses here as well – we return to our soul's home and we shake off the heavy weights and burdens that only assist in keeping us negated and oppressed while we are in the human body vessel.

Do please understand that to keep venturing and returning to walk and enjoy life on earth is a very rich gift and is part of our bigger journey. All of our senses are awakened and we are truly blessed to be able to partake in what is life's greatest gift. We can ultimately achieve enlightenment and awakening on earth. This allows us to enjoy all there is, just on a very different level – physically, where we can see, touch, smell, taste, hear and a multitude of other physical delights, all of which we cannot do or achieve while at rest in the Summerland's.

All that we have been, are now and what we are to enjoy and undertake in our future lives is contained in the Summerlands. When here, we truly and totally connect with our soul on a more intrinsic level – we only sense from a vibrational level, (a lower frequency to our earthly lives) and the only feeling is the most pure sense or feeling that anybody or anything can feel one of utter and total love. Absorbed and held within this place of beauty, we reconnect with ourselves, our family, friends and animals that we have forged connections with throughout time and varying worlds. No longer do we need senses, we just are, and within this we quite simply resonate, and those close to us resonate to and with us. We have now rejoined what is effectively our Soul tribe.

Soul tribe is the term I have used for explaining how, throughout our earthly lives and our return to the Summerlands, we recognise loved ones and friends, but on a very different level – one which is a little difficult to comprehend at times. We will have all met people on our journey through this world who we recognise, communicate with deeply, feel totally at ease with and simply connect with, more so than others. This is our Soul tribe, which forms part of the collective unconscious. A recognition of souls, or energy, that stands the test of time and is not fully explainable, nor always comprehendible, but is undeniable all the same. These are the family, friends and animals we have known and loved ever since our inner soul first emerged at the dawning of time.

Many lifetimes have we journeyed upon and through, and obviously we do not encounter all of these people during our brief stints on earth in one lifetime. However, when we need help or guidance in our physical form, a member of our Soul tribe often appears and the deep recognition is clear to feel within. We cannot deny the connection that we all sense and feel, often without knowing or acknowledging it. It's there though, and it helps us and pushes us onwards to achieve and become the best that we can be. It is this connection, one which is so deep, that urges us on and helps us to live each day and each lifetime, simply because we are not just us, but a diversified puzzle of everyone we have ever known or loved in addition to all our ancestors – quite simply, a multitude of people including every person that has ever come into being. However we take more traits from those with whom we share a deeper connection: our Soul tribe.

Within this sacred space that we return to and recharge, we are surrounded and held in total love – the truest and most pure of any emotion there is. As I have mentioned we don't actually physically sense this, we just resonate and absorb it – an energy exchange of the highest form. Surrounded by only total love, we are free to explore our divine beings inwardly and assess the universe to the highest and most achievable levels that there are. Total and utter calmness, an altered state of being, awareness and serenity in abundance and nothing else. The Summerlands are the perfect place within which to take shelter and solace once our life on earth ends. This is our soul's home and one in which we feel nothing, but understand and comprehend everything. It is here that we totally connect with all there is and become part of everything that the universe has been, is now and will be. It is a perfect stopover point, where we can simply rest and recharge in preparation for our next lifetime and journey.

Over the years I have spoken with many, many people from a multitude of different beliefs, faiths, cultures and religions. Quite often the subject of passing over arises and it's incredible how people of various faiths can and do perceive this event.

One thing that I cannot grasp and will never be able to understand is the way in which some individuals see themselves as above all other life forms. I have spoken with some people and felt deeply saddened by their outlook regarding our fellow creatures. Some actually believe and follow in their religion, or faith, that when an animal passes over, that's it – their light is extinguished and there are no Summerlands, or paradise, for any creature, except if you are human. Personally, I consider this viewpoint totally ludicrous and verging on naivety. It's to say that humankind is above and beyond all other forms of life. To me, this seems to be total ignorance and it's a concept I cannot and will not even contemplate, let alone comprehend.

As with all life, animals are born into this world. These creatures have a spirit and a soul that is so pure that their very arrival, as with any life born, is like a star blinking into life in the night sky. A soul so innocent and untouched that it warms the very essence of anyone privileged enough to witness the natural beauty and amazement of any new life arriving.

All life is born this way. Unfortunately, along the way, humankind can become tainted by various afflictions and worldly trials. Animals are without this. They hold no malice, no ill intention or will. Even when they have been abused, or mistreated, they are happy simply to be. They adjust, learn to trust again and love wholeheartedly and unconditionally, without being tainted at all. An animal will at all costs, and rightly so, protect their offspring or pack, but that's just natural. Apart from this, they act totally without prejudice or bad feeling.

To believe that an animal will never go to the Summerlands is, in my opinion, unbelievable. If there are any beings that may not go there, then it would be humans, but I will touch on that later on. To witness a young animal playing is so precious and beautiful. They are pure and with total innocence, and we can observe this in their behaviour daily. They have no fear – even if they stumble or fall, they get straight back up again and continue on. The sheer resilience of animals is just incredible and an inspiration to us all.

I have myself been witness to much new life emerging – seeing dogs, cats and lambs being born and eggs hatching. All new life is sacred and to be able to hold and cradle any newborn in your arms is a rich gift and a blessing. On the other side, I have held and stroked a life, human and animal, that is slowly ebbing away. Hopefully I have eased their passage and transition into the Summerlands.

Obviously, this transitional time is extremely sad, but to feel, to watch and to be aware and present at the moment the soul departs the body is also a very special and humbling time. To have witnessed this slipping away has, beyond a shadow of a doubt, instilled in me the knowledge that the precious soul within all life will always have a place of peace and rest in the Summerlands.

Attempting to nurse and help an animal back to health is a massive and hard lesson to learn. I have felt like a failure many times in attempting to do this, but on the positive side, I am convinced that I have eased their passing and hopefully comforted them at that time. At the point when a soul leaves and departs the body vessel, total and utter calmness and almost a beauty radiates, which can be both seen and felt. There is no doubt at all in my mind that the purity of animals has shown me that a soul is a soul is a soul, plain and simple. There are no differences at all, whether it is a human or an animal life.

As is the case with the whole of this book, these are my interpretations – shaped by my own unique thoughts, insights and my own personal near death experiences, of which I have had several. This book also reflects the ways in which my guides/ancestors have shown the Summerlands to me.

It appears as a place of love, joy and spiritual abundance. Our loved ones – both humans and animals – reside here after passing over to recharge within the Summerlands. I personally believe that our highest spiritual goal is to gather all the lessons that we can from our many human life experiences, achieve total divinity and then, maybe, we can dwell there permanently. However, this can and will only happen once we have visited this earthly plane as many times as we each have to in order to ultimately achieve purity and attain complete spirituality, therefore becoming the divine beings we are meant to be and are constantly working towards becoming. Only when our whole being is cleansed and free from malice, judgement and negation can we hope to become pure and then remain there, at peace amongst the other divine beings that call the Summerlands home.

This now brings me to another question: are there any beings that may not be permitted to enter – the Summerlands? I believe and know that life and all of creation is made up both in and of total balance – light and dark, male, female, love and hate. On the dark side of the scales of balance, there are and always will be the extremes, just as there are at the lighter end of the spectrum. Unfortunately, there are some truly wretched beings in this world – we all know and are aware of this fact. We could look at this as people who are perhaps having karmic laws played out upon them. We could also consider that we are all on different and varying levels of consciousness/unconsciousness, along with our deeper spiritual awareness. However, I do feel that I have to touch, albeit briefly, on this subject.

To be honest, there are some souls I can only describe as depraved and wretched that exist in this world. People who have preyed on, abused and killed other people, caused immense suffering, created havoc and loss of another's life. Now I am not here to judge another, but this has to be considered. Several of these beings have caused immense pain, mutilation, often torture which has caused the horrendous deaths of others. I find these acts and these individuals so sickening, even to the point of not wanting to contain it within the pages of this book, but I feel that I have to. My consideration of this has brought me to the conclusion that these tormented souls may well not be even allowed to enter the Summerlands, let alone to rest and recharge there. This sacred realm and space simply could not be tarnished by these extremely lost and much damaged beings.

For me to arrive at this conclusion has taken a lot of time, energy and of course, seeking and conversing with my guides and ancestors.

This does not necessarily mean that they won't ever be allowed into the Summerlands; they would have to literally come straight back to earth and into another body vessel, without recharging. I suppose that you could, in a sense liken this about turn without any rest to a form of sleep deprivation. I believe this is a most fitting way for the universal law of karma, which I am sure you will have heard and be aware of, to play itself out in the life of a being who has unfortunately and very sadly fallen into a totally different level, which I will call depraved.

A time to pass over

Undeniably, birth marks the point at which we all undertake a truly amazing and beautiful journey. Quite where this journey will take us or even how long it will last is unknown. The paths we tread are often extremely precarious; tragedy and pitfalls are strewn about and can help us immensely, as we can learn so much from these trials. On the other hand, joy and great elation are in abundance as well, again reflecting the balance that is innate in all creation.

We walk and live several lives within this one. Our paths meander and invariably show and teach us many, many lessons, all of which are invaluable to our inner being, our soul's path and higher awareness and understanding. No one ever said that this journey we are all on would be easy and it certainly isn't. In attuning our spiritual selves, however, we can reach, achieve and attain a more natural and enlightening understanding of just what life is about and what we are ultimately seeking and attempting to achieve.

Lessons that we are given to learn may be of the simplest kind, but these can and often are some of the most difficult to put into practice and truly live by. Both through societal conditioning and the subsequent dumbing down of our species, a great deal of our inherent spirituality may unfortunately be shut down, lost or maybe even extinguished. This is a total travesty and it is up to each one of us, as individuals, to not allow this to happen.

As individuals, we all know right from wrong due a basic instinct. Within this though, we all have free will. It is up to each one of us to embrace, celebrate and rekindle the sacred fire that lies within us all. Upon the awakening from and of our soul, we can then begin to recognise our whole being and ourselves – both the good and the not so good. From this point on, we can under-take the work and constant process of comprehending and understanding the frailties that we each have within ourselves. We can then see how others function, and this can spread out to humankind as a whole.

Yesterday's actions, whether for good or ill, all contain very valuable lessons – ones that we can take with us on our journey. Once we realise this, we can venture further and grasp them and even begin to comprehend ourselves on a much deeper and intricate level. We can then confront exactly who we are, including the darker parts, which we can adapt to and then embrace and use as essential tools on our journey to reach a much more balanced, non judgemental and empathic way of life.

This journey to the Summerlands, which we all find ourselves on, is all about living and ultimately becoming the real you. Life is a very rich and extremely magical gift which we are all blessed to have been granted. We must live it to its fullest potential always, becoming the very best that we can. Enjoy every situation that arises and comes your way. I am a great believer in the universal karmic law. We get back what we give out, so we need to only give out and resonate outwardly that which we would like to receive. Ultimately, we are what lies inside us. Live it, love it and become it.

Several times in my life I have experienced what I believe to be the beginning of the process of passing over into the Summerlands. Basically, there have been times when I should have died. However, I am still here and extremely happy to be, be it through sheer luck at times – it obviously is not my time to pass over. I totally cherish and enjoy each and every second of being alive on this beautiful earth and embrace every opportunity that comes my way.

I have slumped and started to fade away on more than one occasion. Upon doing so, the exact same feelings have washed over me each time. Total and utter warmth and feelings of complete euphoria like you cannot imagine. Total contentedness and a resonance of belonging, and feeling at one and at peace with everything to such an extent that to come back to my earthly body was a shock.

There is a time for everything and everything has a time. This is and can be a very hard lesson to grasp, let alone learn, but if and when we manage to figure it out, life does become so much easier and more harmonious. We can then begin to go with the flow and become, on all levels, part of the universe's greater plan.

Once our body does finally give out and expire, the process of the soul leaving and making its transition to the Summerlands is one that I envisage like this. As the soul departs the body, it feels as though all of the elements (earth, air, fire and water) purify, cleanse and wash over us – which could explain the feelings of euphoria that I myself and others have experienced at times of near death. The God that exists in all creation then comes to collect your soul. The God of the trees, stars, rivers, animals, minerals and all that exists, comforts, reassures and then, in all his might, power and empathy, cradles you in his arms, carries you away and gently lays you at the feet of the Goddess. Once at her feet, your passageway into the Summerlands is complete.

This experience, as I see it, is our ultimate journey and all part of our soul's learning, awakening and progression. This is the journey upon which we are all embarking and undertaking from the moment of birth.

In February of 2015, my Mum passed away. She had been poorly for a while, so her death was expected, but this was still a very hard and stressful time. My Mum held onto life in a hospital in Essex for just over three weeks until her passing, which just goes to show the strength and sheer resilience of the human spirit and soul. The night before my Mum was taken into hospital, she had phoned me, as happened on a regular basis. Within a few seconds of starting the conversation, I realised that it wasn't my Mums usual manner in talking with me. It then clicked and I became aware that my Mum was talking to me from her soul. This had never happened before and I know that it was such a blessing to have had this, what was to be our final conversation before she passed away into the Summerlands.

We spoke, listened and both cried during this chat, as my Mum explained she was tired and wanted to go home. In all my life, I have never had such a heightened communication with anyone and my Mum was one of the last people I would have ever expected to have had such a spiritual talk with even at the best of times. My Mum knew she was fading and she had phoned me to literally say goodbye.

The next morning, as her next of kin, I received a phone call to say that she had been rushed into hospital and wasn't expected to last the day. Obviously, this was a very hard time and I gained lots of strength from that last conversation that we had together. As the days turned into weeks and my Mum was holding onto life, I started thinking that I should make the long trip to go and see her. Each time I felt this, I knew that if I went, all that would happen was that I would work as and anchor and keep her in this world. So, as difficult as it was, I did not visit, but instead imagined her in a small boat, slowly being carried further and further out by the waves. I knew that at some point, the inevitable phone call would come to say that my Mum had finally passed away.

Just after midnight on the 9 February 2015, the hospital rang me to say she was drawing her last breath and she passed peacefully as I was on the phone. I hold no regrets for not visiting her as I know that the enlightening talk we had 3 weeks earlier was a very special and sacred moment and I hold that dear to me. I know that I was very blessed to have that special time to say farewell and just listen and comfort her.

As I have mentioned before in this book, those we have loved, our family and friends, they are with us and are a part of who we are. We not only live this life for ourselves, for our own learning and experiences, but also for these beautiful souls that have already left and journeyed to the Summerlands. We owe them so much and without them, we would not be who we are today.

They have not gone, they have just moved address, changed their phone number and we cannot visit them. Within this, they inspire and walk with us every day. Our hearts are full of the memories we have of them so, while we carry them in our hearts, they are not gone and remain with us always – we just communicate with them on a very different level and in a different way.

> I am the embrace of the breeze you feel around
> you.
> I am the cool waters that wash over and cleanse
> you.
> The fire you feel inside you, it is me, as I urge you
> on.
> I am the solid earth you walk upon and holds you.
> I have not gone, just moved on. I am within and
> around you always.

As with any period of change, or transition, we can become very anxious and worried. There is no need to worry at all – upon our calling, when it is our time to pass over, all fear will be removed. We will be cleansed and will almost be longing to go home to the Summerlands.

Our soul knows where we are from and where we are heading upon death. When our time does come, all the knowledge, wisdom and thoughts will once again be collected and put within our conscious and unconscious being. Our very own personal databank of experiences will be processed and imprinted upon our soul and very essence. All of this is in readiness for the next journey we are to undertake, wherever that may take us.

We only find ourselves nervous due to the constraints and restraints that are placed upon us by society and our own fears. Too often, these fears are forced upon us by our parents, peers and others. Upon awakening and the realisation that we are all as one and a part of the universe as a whole, these fears will often be dispelled and erased. For our own sense of being and completeness within, we need to cut the ties that bind us and alleviate and remove fear, which only serves as a way to restrict us physically, mentally and spiritually. If we are to maybe attain a higher state of being and consciousness, we must have total and complete trust in who we are, the universe and creation as a whole. We have to look deep within to find this and to work with and understand all of this. Once we can achieve this, we are so much freer and more deeply aware of everything within the world and other worlds and realms.

We are everything and we are infinite beings, just not in this body vessel. We live our lives like chapters in a book, slowly building up a whole and complete story. When it is our time to pass, we must accept and embrace it. The best is always yet to come. Now, I do not wish to pass yet – I love this life and all that comes with it – but I have no fear at all of my passing into the Summerlands. I just hope that it is not for many more years to come.

A time to recharge and rest

We have now entered the Summerlands. Basically, this is the place where our spiritual self comes to rest and recharge, to explore and learn from our last life's lessons – to evaluate them and to evolve once again. Similar to a battery that needs recharging, this resting period is essential to our very being. Only here can we truly understand and comprehend the physical journey and lessons that we have endured.

As the swirling vortex we are in the Summerlands – simply because we are not held within a body vessel – we return once more to just being pure and unadulterated energy. This is a time of freedom where we are not restrained, but free to rest and make plans for the next journey we will undertake when we visit earth once more – in another guise, but joined by the same soul, our soul.

It is within this period of recharging and rest that we choose our next chapter, the next journey, the next life and we decide which blueprint we are going to follow to allow and help us learn and achieve the lessons we need to awaken and enlighten our soul's progression further.

There is not an allotted time frame there and it wouldn't be relevant anyway. Who knows how long we stay there to rest? It might be days, months, years, or even centuries – it simply does not matter.

A time of connecting once more with our Soul tribe is vital here as well. Family members, loved ones, animals and friends who have passed are here and we all recognise one another, just from a different level. We feel each other from a much lower vibrational level than most of us can truly comprehend, having been used to life in a physical body. Once we are no longer encased within that, our soul leads the way and resonates with loved ones and like minded beings. As I mentioned earlier, we have no bodies here, and we therefore have none of the senses that physicality brings. We are totally devoid of our earthly traits and we become and revert back to the base level of existence, which is vibration, where we just feel and sense. This is a totally pure and raw form of the energy within us all.

It is the Yuletide period of 2015 as I write this section, a time of festivities, families and friends coming together and celebrating.

I have just heard the devastating news that my friend Grahame Smith has tragically died. He died on December 22nd, just as he was coming home from seeing one of his favourite bands performing. This just reinstalls within me once again, the fragility of life and how we must never take anything or anyone for granted. In a heartbeat, or lack of it, any one of us can pass away and for those left behind, the world seems empty and devoid of that person.

I never met Grahame in person, but met him on a social media site five years ago. We messaged regularly and had several common interests. Grahame loved music, he was a DJ and his zest for life was incredible.

He loved his family and he shared his love for Bulgaria with me and we spoke of that often. He was going to move out there in February 2016 with his partner Gillian. Now that will not happen and Gillian will be feeling destroyed by this sudden and cruel turn of events – her world will never be the same again.

Grahame's passion and love for life was truly inspirational. He loved my writings and was looking forward to me completing this book, so it's only fitting, that such a kind, honourable and respectful man, friend and someone I called my Brother, should get a mention within these pages. As I shed tears for a loss, I also gain strength and inspiration knowing that a place has already been reserved in the Summerlands, for this beautiful soul, who was loved and adored by so many. Thank you Grahame, for everything – not just what you did for me, but for many, many people. R.I.P. Grahame Smith.

When any death occurs, it creates ripples throughout the world and those closest feel the effects the most. However we view the stages of death, it is a very traumatic and sad time. The grieving process is a harrowing period to which there are many stages. Senses of loss, guilt, anger, love and sadness are to name but a few of those felt. Every death will bring about different emotions and no two losses are ever felt the same. However many deaths we witness, to lose a family member, friend, partner, or pet never gets any easier. Within this time of sadness, we should look back at the lessons we have learnt from this person and remember them fondly. While we do this, we are living for them and they are partaking in our daily lives and inspiring us constantly. We are them, as they are us.

Upon reflection, I can look back upon my life and see that I have walked within the realm and shadow of death, or passing over, ever since I was first born, way back in 1969. I find this fascinating when I now reflect upon this – not in a morbid sense, but a sense of total and utter joy. Without all these experiences, I would not fully appreciate life and if we fail to appreciate anything, then sadly, we can become nonchalant, complacent and that can then lead to us taking things for granted. We have all been guilty of this at times, but to fully enjoy everything we have, we must savour every moment and never take anything for granted – not for one single moment.

As we now start to become more aware, as a race, of our physicality, our minds and our souls, I believe that we are becoming more attuned and heightened as a whole. Society can be extremely draconian and I am seeing more and more people reaching the understanding and coming to the realisation that we are infinite beings. We need now to step out of the controlled mindset that we all too often find ourselves in the grip of. An awakening is happening across the world now, more so than ever before. More and more people are seeking an alternative, a more peaceful way of life and existence and that can only be reached and achieved once we look and venture deep within ourselves.

As I have mentioned before, we are all spiritual beings, merely having a human existence. Upon the understanding and the awareness of being and living a spiritual life, our whole way of thinking, feeling and the way in which we approach our day to day lives totally changes. Across the spectrum, a more harmonious way to live is being looked into and explored by millions of people. It's as if we, as a collective, are now reverting back to the older and more natural ways – the ways that our ancestors would have lived, celebrated and enjoyed.

For our very existence and to attain a more natural and pleasant way to live, we have to venture and delve into what makes us tick and brings us the greatest joy. Upon the awareness and appreciation that true riches are not found outside of us, but within our very essence, our core and soul, then maybe, just maybe, the long awaited shift to a more compassionate and empathic way for mankind to live and exist together in love and peace can be reached and achieved.

As a whole, we should no longer need to treat death as the taboo subject which it is often viewed as. We should instead see it as a re-birth and not an ending. When there is a birth, we celebrate the arrival of a new life; why then, don't we celebrate a passing over?

Life ends and it is a terribly sad, traumatic and emotional time, especially for those closest. This is when we need to see the positives of that person's life. We have been blessed and enriched by simply knowing them and sharing time and our journey together. We must look back and remember fondly how enriching their very presence was, the love that was shared, the tender moments and utter joy that they bought in and gave to our lives. These are the sacred and precious moments we were lucky enough to exchange with them. Their very being and existence has taught and shown us so much and we have been honoured to have walked and trodden their path with them.

A life ends, but it is never goodbye, it's simply farewell, as we wish them a peaceful transition to the Summerlands – the place we go to rest and recharge, until we are born once more, to start a new life and learn more lessons.

I am not gone, I have just moved on.
I am within and around you always.
Feel me, hear me and sense me, for I am here.
I watch over you in all you do. Call my name and
I will answer you, a message I will send.
Remember me fondly and often. I am you, as you
    are me.
Carry me in your heart and I will always be with
    you.

When a death occurs

Around the world and from country to country, the procedures which have to be followed and adhered to when a death has happened obviously change. Here are some helpful pointers and legal procedures from the UK.

When any of us suffer bereavement, a cremation or burial for a member of the family, or a close friend, is the most difficult day of your life. All the emotions and feelings that are ever felt or thought about a loved one are expressed on that day.

Funeral directors are a great starting point and with qualified, friendly and efficient staff, this immensely hard time, can often be eased considerably. These people can take the burden and stress away and tailor make a funeral/ cremation to your wishes, or follow the person's will (if they made one) or funeral plan accordingly.

Registering a death is usually the first thing to do; nothing can happen until the death has been registered. If the death occurs within a hospital, apply to the hospital (not your family doctor) for the Medical Certificate of Death.

In cases where the death has been reported to the coroner, the procedure is somewhat different. The coroner and his/hers officers are working in your interest. No doctor will issue a Medical Certificate of Death. This will be sent by the coroner to the Registrar's Office in the district where the death occurred, after contact has been made with the Coroner's Office.

To register a death is quite a harrowing experience, especially for a loved one, but unfortunately, it is essential. Those who can register a death are a close relative of the deceased; a relative in attendance during last illness; a relative living in the district where the death occurred; or the person who is disposing of the body.

The documents that are required to register a death are a Medical Certificate of Death and the deceased's medical card, if available, or the birth certificate and information regarding the date of birth.

The information required to register a death is as follows: date and place of death; the full name of the deceased (maiden name if applicable); date and place of birth; occupation; and home address. If the deceased was married, the full name and occupation of their surviving spouse is needed also.

Consulting a solicitor may be an option as well, especially if they have copies of the deceased's will or there are problems with intestacy, outstanding debts and other considerations. A solicitor could, as well as easing the worry and stress, also save you money. A person's will is often placed in the hands of a solicitor, or could be placed in the home, among personal paperwork, or may be with their bank for safe keeping.

For anybody that loses a loved one, it is an extremely emotional, sad and very tough time – my heart goes out to anybody that experiences this. Unfortunately, we all will at some time and I can only hope that you may find some comfort and solace within these pages.

A funeral director will accommodate and take the deceased's wishes, or the next of kin's wishes, if a will was not made. They will walk you through every step of what will happen and what is required legally. Floral tributes, favourite songs, type of funeral, burial or cremation, maybe donations to a chosen charity, what type of ceremony – all of these things and more have to be decided on and put into place.

Alternative funerals are becoming more common-place nowadays. This means that a fitting funeral can be arranged according to the deceased's belief system, where they can be celebrated in their time of transition in a way that best honours how they lived and led their lives. Once again, funeral directors will be able to show you all of the different options available and will accommodate accordingly.

As I have pointed out and mentioned numerous times in this book, death is a very traumatic experience for those left behind. For the deceased, it's the beginning of another chapter in their book of lives and living. No matter what, respect, honour and love should always be shown and their final wishes should be followed accordingly. For those left behind to mourn, a funeral provides closure and an inner peace often follows. To celebrate the life of a loved one, close friend or family member is the best way to gain this closure. In doing so, you are honouring the person totally by remembering and celebrating their life. There is no better way to do this than to see friends and family at the immensely sad time that surrounds a death – to all gather and celebrate the life they lived and shared is deeply touching and very humbling indeed.

Any death, or passing over is a deeply felt and heart wrenching time – I know that, have felt it and witnessed it many times. I am not in any way at all detracting from anybody's loss and I have total understanding, compassion and empathy for anybody that loses a loved one, or friend, I really do. What I am trying to do, is to give an alternate way to view this whole process, so that we are not fearful of death and can maybe reach a point of understanding where – that through the tears, loss and heartbreak – we can see the whole and bigger picture. To know, deep within, that it is another vital stage of our soul's journey to becoming complete and at peace with all of creation, is where we can see death from a different viewpoint and stance.

We celebrate birth – let's start celebrating a passing. In doing so, we can join together with family and friends; we can remember fondly how that person touched and warms our lives and hearts. We can gather together and recognise, appreciate and celebrate the life that has now left this mortal earth and journeyed onwards to new beginnings, and transitioned to a new beginning and rebirth. Just as the train and its carriages moves on and departs from one station to another, our life's journey is the same.

They have not gone; they have just moved addresses. We no longer know where they live and we have no phone number to contact them on. They are always with us, around and within us and there in all that we do. If we feel and listen, we know they are here. We are them, as they are us. Gone, never forgotten and always in our hearts, this is where they now live.

Writing this book has taken me on an incredible journey. Not only have I answered some of my own questions while doing this, but several questions have arisen that I am slowly getting answers for and I have no doubt that they all will be answered at some time. I hope you have enjoyed reading what is effectively my interpretation on this subject. I also hope it has been of comfort to you.

Please feel free to contact me via e-mail.
spiritoftheawen@yahoo.com

I wish you all much peace and joy
on your life's journey.

Blessings and much love to you all.

Playlist

Whilst writing this book, there have been times of despair, when I felt lost and was struggling to put down into words the thoughts and feelings I had. At times, I have written with total silence, through day and night and all hours. Mostly, I have had music on in the background and the inspiration gained from this has helped me immensely so I feel it is only right to give this a mention. I find that music feeds the soul and invigorates us on all levels – mentally, physically and spiritually. The list compiled here covers a wide range of genres, but these artists and bands have, without them knowing, helped me create and write this book. Many thanks.

Radio 2 at various times, assorted artists

James Blunt

Paul Weller in his various guises: The Jam,
The Style Council, and as a soloist

The Verve

Gabrielle

Maggie Beth Sand and her band Serpentyne

Adele

Crowded House

James Bay

Coldplay

Loreena McKennitt

Clannad

Enya

Eva Cassidy

There was a lot of music listened to during the writing of this book, but the above were the main inspiration. Many thanks.